JASON VALE

the Juice Master

little book of simple smoothies

HarperThorsons
An Imprint of HarperCollins*Publishers*
77–85 Fulham Palace Road,
Hammersmith, London W6 8JB

The website address is: www.thorsonselement.com

and *HarperThorsons* are trademarks
of HarperCollins*Publishers* Ltd

First published by HarperThorsons 2007

The text in this book was first published in
The Juice Master Turbo-charge Your Life in 14 Days
and *The Juice Master Keeping it Simple*

10 9 8 7 6 5 4 3 2 1

Juice Master is a registered trademark and all the
Juice Boost supplements are copyright to the author

Jason Vale asserts the moral right to
be identified as the author of this work

A catalogue record of this book is available
from the British Library

ISBN-13 978-0-00-722517-0
ISBN-10 0-00-722517-2

Printed and bound in China by
Imago

Contents

Pure Smoothie Power

It's official — smoothies are the new black! If a drink or food could ever be classed as a fashion accessory then smoothies would be the new Prada on the block. For the first time in history, it is now trendier for students to hold a Strawberry Sunrise than it is to hold a margarita. The UK alone drank a whopping 34 million litres of smoothies in 2006, compared to just 6.3 million in 2001. Yep, there is no doubt about it, juices and smoothies are the fastest-growing sector in the soft-drinks market (just behind water), and this means we are all getting healthier — right? Well the simple answer is um — NO!

Not All Smoothies Are What They Seem

Little Book of Simple Smoothies is my small opportunity to give you an insight into the 'health tricks' of the smoothie world. At least when you buy a sugar-loaded soda, you know what you are getting. But when it comes to smoothies and juices you assume you're getting something healthy. However, not all the apparent 'pure' bottle or carton juices and smoothies on the shelves are what they seem. There are even health tricks going on in many juice-bar chains up and down the country. All of which will make you see why making a mouth-watering smoothie at home is often the only way to guarantee a genuinely healthy smoothie for you and the little ones.

The Heat Is On

The vast majority of shop-bought smoothies are flash pasteurized. 'Flash Pasteurization' is a process where the life-giving liquid from nature's finest is subjected to temperatures of 71.5°C (160°F) to 74°C (165°F), for about 15 to 30 seconds. This may not seem like a disaster, but the heat lowers the vitamin and mineral content and destroys the enzyme activity. Enzymes are the life-force contained within nature's plant foods and the main reason I make juices and smoothies at home. Enzymes are the 'X factor', and sometimes all the scientific research in the world cannot fully explain nature's amazing ability to protect, heal and nourish when food is taken in its most natural state. Pasteurized may be better in terms of shelf life, but when we're talking about what is best for us, freshly made will always beat pasteurized hands down.

Fable Label

We are often told we shouldn't believe all we read, and that certainly holds true when looking at the misleading headline labels on many juices and smoothies. I recently bought a bottled smoothie with '**A Is For Acai**' on the label. Acai (pronounced ah-sci-ee) berries are said to contain more anti-oxidants than any other fruit on earth, so I assumed I was buying a smoothie rich in the Amazon super berry. But when I looked at the label closely, things weren't what they seemed. Here are the ingredients in the order they appear – apple juice from concentrate (47%), banana purée (35%), blackcurrant purée (9%), blueberry purée (5%), Acai pulp (water, citric acid) (4%). So a smoothie which has the massive headline '**A** IS FOR … **ACAI** the new "super" berry! **ANTIOXIDANTS** to keep you healthy' contains in reality less than 5% of the super berry. The vast bulk is made up of **concentrated** apple juice! This particular smoothie even has an 'antioxidant fruit comparison' chart to illustrate that Acai berries are probably the most anti-oxidant-rich fruit in the world. This small dark purple fruit is indeed one of nature's true super foods, but this smoothie is not loaded with Acai but concentrated apple juice, some purée and a miniscule amount of Acai. And not only is the juice pasteurized, but 47% of the drink is also from concentrate. Still not concerned?

But I Am Guaranteed A Healthy Smoothie At A Juice Bar – Right?

You'd think. Unfortunately, even when the smoothie is being made right before your eyes, things aren't always what they seem. Be wary of signs such as, 'We Use 98% **Fat-Free Live Yogurt**'. 'Fat free' doesn't mean 'refined-sugar free'. I was in a juice bar in Ireland and was shocked to discover that the 'fat-free' yogurt was absolutely loaded with **SUGAR** and **GLUCOSE SYRUP** (which is more sugar), and only 40% of the whole thing was **actually** yogurt: 60% was made up with chemicals, refined sugars and other rubbish – none of which were any relation to yogurt! Refined sugar will store itself in the body as FAT unless you burn it off! And the 'live' claim is often extremely tenuous. When a yogurt is frozen, the vast majority of live cultures die. So there may be a tiny percentage that still remains live, but the amount is only good for the label – not so much for your gut! Also, keep your eyes open for the old 'pasteurized juice into the smoothie' trick. This is cleverly done by putting some frozen fruits into a blender and then adding some pasteurized juice from a dispenser or carton in the back. My advice on this one is clear. When you are in any juice bar, look for the pasteurized juice, ask if the yogurt is frozen and sugar-loaded, and don't be fooled by the fresh fruit on display. But don't worry – there are still some great juice bars around where you can get extremely healthy juices and smoothies, see www.juicemaster.com for details.

Does This Mean All Smoothies In The Shops Are Bad?

NO! Many, like the 'Innocent' brand still have vitamins, minerals, some good fats, amino acids and sugars. No way on earth could smoothies of this nature ever be described as 'bad'. However, even these are nowhere near the, 'no heat applied' super healthy smoothies you can make at home.

'if You Can't Eat it – Drink it!'

Talking good health is one thing, doing it is another. This is why I am a huge fan of home juicing and smoothie making. Many people just don't get around to eating enough raw fruit and vegetables and the quickest and easiest way to get your daily dose of natural vitamins, minerals, natural fats and natural sugars is to put them in a blender, add some freshly extracted juice, blend into a smoothie and drink it. I honestly believe that without the ease of juicing and smoothie making, I would still be an extremely overweight guy covered from head to foot in psoriasis and desperately trying to breathe through bad asthma. Now, I have nature, a juicer, and a blender to thank for my good health. My asthma is history, the fat has melted away and my psoriasis has receded. In short, the smoothies you will be creating are far from simply 'drinks'. They are without question the best health insurance you will ever invest in. And speaking of investment, in order to get yourself well and truly juiced (or smoothied – if there is such a word), you will need…

The Right Juicy Kit

There is nothing more important to long-term home juice and smoothie making than getting the right kit. Let's be honest, juicing and smoothie making have been given a bad rap over the years in terms of hassle. As healthy as they may be, making a juice or a smoothie used to be 'a pain in the proverbial'!

Broadband Juicing

The good news is that juice extractors and smoothie makers have come a long way in the last few years and we have progressed from what I call, 'old dial-up connection' equipment, to 'BROADBAND'. Broadband juicing and smoothie making is here and that means SPEED! The biggest obstacle which would turn people off from juicing and making a super smoothie was time. Juicing in particular was incredibly time consuming. These days, wide-chute juicers, more extraction, large pulp containers for continuous juicing, and dishwasher-safe machines have made juicing fast and easy. There are now some juicers on the market that can even fit 3 whole apples at once with no chopping or peeling – that's heaven if you have ever juiced with an old 'dial-up' juicer in the past. One such machine is the new Philips Alu Juicer. By the time you read this book, they may have changed the model, but I hope not. After all when something is excellent, why change it? At the time of writing this book, the model known as The Aluminium Juicer by Philips was voted into the 'Best Buy' section of a **Which?** Magazine test on juicers, won 'Best Juicer' in **Good Housekeeping**, and scored 10 out of 10 in a **Daily Mirror** test of all juicers. Although this little book is all about smoothie making, you should consider getting a juicer to add the liquid element. You can just add some carton or bottled juice and mix with fresh fruit, but after the intro you may want to do things the healthiest and tastiest way. If you are going to invest in a juicer – the Philips Alu Juicer is the one to get. Things are always changing and improving though, so check out www.juicemaster.com to see what's new in the juicing world.

Smoothie Makers

Let me point something out here – a blender **is** a smoothie maker. If you own a blender then you own a smoothie maker! Since you probably already own a smoothie maker, you just need to make sure it's built for the job at hand. Not all blenders are built the same, and you need one that will blend ice, frozen fruits and vegetables like mango and avocado with ease. There are a ton of blenders on the market, and many are extremely good. If you have the Philips Alu Juicer then, even if it's only for aesthetic purposes, I would get the Philips Alu Blender. This blender not only matches the juicer, but it's an extremely good smoothie maker as well. It has a separate 'smoothie' button which makes for easy smoothie making.

Always check www.juicemaster.com for the latest recommendations or give our juicy team a call on 08451 30 28 29 (low call rate from anywhere in the UK) if you have questions. We're always happy to help.

Recipes

simply divine

Freshly extracted **orange** juice **blended** together with **fresh strawberries, mango** and crushed **ice**

Picture lying on a white sandy beach, the sun beating down, and sipping an ice-cold creamy fruit cocktail. If you close your eyes when drinking this divine smoothie, it is possible to forget where you are and transport yourself for a few minutes.

1 **orange** (peeled but with pith on)
1 small handful **strawberries**
1 **mango** (de-stoned)
1 small handful crushed **ice**

Juice the orange. Put the strawberries, mango and ice
in the blender along with the juice. Blend – pour – enjoy!

Smoothie benefits Rich in vitamins B, C and E, and
loaded with zinc, iron, calcium and potassium. The zinc helps to
maintain the proper concentration of vitamin E in the blood.
The natural sugars give an energy lift.

tropical paradise

Fresh **pineapple** juice, puréed **banana** and luscious **mango**, blended with cool **coconut** milk

Quite simply paradise in a glass!

2 inch slice medium size **pineapple**
¼ peeled **banana**
¼ **mango** (de-stoned)
½ mug **coconut milk** (straight from the coconut for preference, otherwise organic/fairtrade from shop)

1 handful crushed **ice**

Juice the pineapple and pour into blender. Add the banana, mango, coconut milk and ice. Blend – pour – enjoy!

Smoothie benefits This tropical delight is bursting with potassium – which is important for a healthy nervous system and regular heart rhythm. This mineral alone helps to prevent stroke, aids proper muscle contraction and works with sodium to control the body's water balance. Also rich in vitamins B and C, folic acid, magnesium, 'good' fats, iron and calcium. Coconut milk is also low in calories!

natural
protein shake

Nature's finest extracted pure apple juice, blended with fresh, ripe banana and scrummy blueberries

This really is Mother Nature's protein power punch. No unnatural 'protein' powders, artificial amino acids or scary steroids are to be found in this protein-packed smoothie. It is bursting with flavour as well as oozing essential amino acids — the body's building blocks for protein.

2 **apples** (Golden Delicious or Royal Gala for preference)
½ **banana** (fairtrade if possible)
1 handful fresh **blueberries**
1 small handful crushed **ice**

Juice the apples. Put the banana, blueberries and ice along with apple juice in the blender. Blend – pour – enjoy!

Smoothie benefits Bananas have four times the protein, twice the carbohydrate, three times the phosphorus, five times the vitamin A and twice the other vitamins and minerals than apples. Not bad when you think that apples are loaded with vitamins A, B2, B3, B6 and C, as well as being one of the most nutritionally rich foods on the planet. Blueberries are one of nature's superfoods and are also loaded with amino acids – the building blocks for protein. A true protein power food.

banana 'n' honey zest

Creamy **banana** combined with **fresh OJ** and a hint of nature's finest **mouth-watering** Manuka active **honey**

This combination works perfectly together, with the creaminess of the banana and the sweetness of the honey subtly balancing the tanginess of the fresh OJ.

2 juicy **oranges**
½ ripe **banana**
1 teaspoon **Manuka active honey**
(or whichever variety you have)

1 small handful **ice**

Peel the oranges, leaving as much of the white pith as possible (as this is where most of the vitamins and nutrients are to be found). Simply juice the oranges and pour into the blender with the banana, honey and ice. Blend – pour – enjoy!

Smoothie benefits
Bananas are one of the best sources of potassium, essential for maintaining normal blood pressure and heart function. The banana delivers a perfect source of slow release energy, while the honey gives a much quicker energy fix. If you're a sports enthusiast or looking for a quick pick-me-up, you will love the potassium-power delivered by this high energy smoothie.

breakfast on the move

This is an alternative to the ever so popular Breakfast on the Go found in our Juice Master Juice 'n' Smoothie bars. You can use any berries you like but the combination of strawberries and raspberries works particularly well.

1 handful fresh **strawberries**
1 handful fresh **raspberries**
50g low-fat live **yogurt**
50g **soya milk**
50g **muesli** (no added sugar/salt)
1 small handful **ice cubes**

Place all the ingredients in the blender. Blend — enjoy!

Smoothie benefits If your usual breakfast is a couple of slices of white, nutrient-devoid toast with full-fat butter and sugar-loaded jam, then your body and waistline are in for a real treat. Replacing your regular breakfast with this delicious alternative will not only cut out the fat and artificial sugar, but will also supply the body with a huge dollop of goodness. The raspberries and strawberries contain a distinguished array of vitamins, minerals and anti-oxidants that boost the immune system as well as destroy free radical damage. The friendly bacteria found in the low-fat live yogurt furnishes the intestine with 'good' bacteria to aid digestion and fight bad bacterial infections. Muesli provides a great source of dietary fibre, minerals, vitamins and natural sugar. This smoothie is bursting with goodness and will certainly keep you filled up till lunchtime!

salad smoothie

Rich **avocado**, accompanied by water-rich **cucumber**, sodium-rich **celery**, apple, sweet baby leaf **spinach** and **watercress**

We don't always get around to eating enough salads, so it's nice to know you can always drink one!

- 2 **apples** (Golden Delicious or Royal Gala are best)
- 1 inch chunk medium **cucumber**
- ½ stick **celery**
- 1 generous handful **baby leaf spinach**
- 1 small handful **watercress**
- ½ ripe **avocado** (organic if possible)
- 4 **ice cubes** or a small handful **crushed ice**

Juice the apples, cucumber, celery, spinach and watercress. Add the flesh of the avocado to the blender along with the juice and ice. Blend – pour – marvel at the miracle that is salad in a glass!

Smoothie benefits It is thought that avocados are the only food on the planet which you could live on exclusively. They contain essential fats, natural sugars, amino acids (nature's body builders), vitamins, minerals, organic water and enzymes. Spinach juice is rich in nature's liquid sunshine – chlorophyll – as well as beta-carotene, folic acid, iron, choline and vitamins A, C and E. Add the rest of the ingredients and you have all the goodness of a salad, but in a liquid form.

berry beauty

Deep, **dark**, mysterious **blueberries** and **blackberries**, carefully combined with the freshly **extracted** juice of **two** sweet **apples** and a **generous** helping of creamy live **yogurt**

The rich colour and intensity of the berries combined with the smooth, silky texture of the yogurt make this smoothie utterly delicious.

2 **apples** (Golden Delicious or Royal Gala are best)
1 handful **blueberries**
1 handful **blackberries**
200g low-fat live **yogurt**
1 handful **ice** cubes

Juice the apples. Put the blueberries, blackberries, yogurt and ice into the blender with the apple juice. Blend – pour – enjoy!

Smoothie benefits The berries are bursting with anti-oxidants, vitamins B, C, E and K, calcium, iron, magnesium and phosphorus. What's more, they contain ellagic acid, which is a phytochemical that is believed to slow down the signs of ageing. So this really is a very berry beauty!

pure peachy passion

The soft tender flesh from the ripe peach is perfectly united with the sub-tropical, aromatic flavour of the mysterious passion fruit. This distinctive, unique, fleshy purple fruit has a musky, sweet, yet tart flavour, which is flawlessly balanced by the soft, understated taste of the delicate peach – umm peachy!

2 **apples** (Golden Delicious or Royal Gala are best)
1 ripe **peach**
1 **passion fruit**
1 small handful **ice**

Simply wash and juice the apples. Gently cut the flesh away from the peach and place in the blender. Cut the passion fruit in half and scoop the flesh out into the blender. Add the apple juice and ice. Blend – pour – enjoy!

Smoothie benefits Passion fruit has been the staple diet of people in the Amazon rainforest for eons. South American indigenous tribes believe this unique fruit offers many healing properties and is most notably used as a heart tonic. It is also a great source of vitamins A and C as well as containing high levels of potassium. Vitamin B3 (niacin) found in the peach helps lower cholesterol and improve circulation.

raspberry fizzle

Fresh **raspberries** and **yogurt** blended **together** with a **touch** of **fizz** and **ice**

The gentle bubbles of naturally carbonated water adds a subtle fizzle to this juicy raspberry smoothie.

1 large handful **raspberries**
50g low-fat live **yogurt**
100ml mineral **water**
(any fizzy mineral water is good but Perrier is best)
4 **ice cubes** or a handful **crushed ice**

No need for your juicer — just your blender! Place all ingredients into the blender. Blend — pour — enjoy the fizzy edge to this sharp smoothie!

Smoothie benefits Raspberries may not be classed in the same superfood bracket as blueberries, acai or goji, but they are still packed with vitamins C and E, calcium, magnesium, phosphorus, sodium, ellagic acid, fibre, zinc, iron and antioxidants. This smoothie is excellent for maintaining a proper water balance and blood pH, and it helps good kidney function and is excellent for bones and teeth.

nutty blueberry cream

Smooth, creamy, buttery almonds, combined with decadent blueberries and accompanied by thick live yogurt

This deep vibrant blue opulent smoothie is not only delicious with a capital D but it's also a smoothie you can get your teeth into.

1 **apple** (Royal Gala or Golden Delicious are best)
1 small handful **almonds** (soaked overnight)
50g low-fat live **yogurt** (if vegan use soya yogurt)
1 small handful **blueberries** (fresh or frozen)
4 **ice cubes** or a small handful **crushed ice**

Juice the apple and pour into the blender. Add all the other ingredients. Blend till smooth – pour – love the nuts!

Smoothie benefits High in essential good fats, extremely alkalizing and loaded with anti-oxidants, potassium, vitamins, minerals and amino acids. Almonds are also high in calcium, making this smoothie an excellent one for healthy bones and teeth.

cranberry 'n' orange

Freshly extracted orange juice blended with cranberries, bananas and ice

Cranberries have an instantly refreshing flavour that beautifully complements the zestiness of freshly extracted orange juice. This perfect partnership, combined with creamy puréed banana and crushed ice, means this smoothie is as refreshing as it is delicious!

2 medium **oranges** (peeled – leave as much pith on as possible)

1 small handful **cranberries** (fresh or frozen)

½ **banana** (fairtrade if possible)

4 **ice cubes** or a small handful **crushed ice**

Juice the oranges and add to the blender. Add the cranberries, banana and ice. Blend – pour – and enjoy!

Smoothie benefits Cranberry juice contains something called quininic acid, better known as quinine. Quininic acid is so powerful that it converts to another acid that helps to lift toxins not only from the bladder and kidneys but also from the prostate and testicles. Cranberries also have vitamins A and C, iodine, calcium, beta-carotene, folic acid, magnesium, phosphorus and potassium in them.

fruit 'n' nut case

Freshly extracted **apple** juice combined with mixed **nuts**, mixed **fruit** and **yogurt**

This should satisfy the desires of even the most diehard fruit and nut heads. This is a smoothie that you can actually get your teeth into. The trick is not to blend it for too long — that way you can still enjoy chewing on the occasional nut or juicy raisin.

2 **apples** (Royal Gala or Golden Delicious are best)
1 small handful **almonds** (soaked overnight)
1 small handful **brazil nuts**
1 small handful **cashews**
1 small handful **raisins**
1 small handful **mixed frozen fruit**
2 tablespoons low-fat live **yogurt**

Juice the apples and pour into the blender. Add the nuts, raisins, mixed fruit and yogurt to the blender. Blend quickly — pour — and enjoy!

Smoothie benefits Loaded with zinc, selenium, essential fats, protein and calcium. Raisins are rich in natural sugars and vitamins and the live yogurt will help replace friendly bacteria in the gut and slow the absorption of sugars in the bloodstream. It also contains vitamins A, B1, B2, B6 and C, beta-carotene, iron, magnesium, phosphorus, potassium, sulphur, pectin and malic acid.

savoury sweet

Rich, creamy organic **avocado** combined with the **sweet** taste of **freshly** extracted **apple** juice and zesty natural **lime** juice

2 **apples** (Golden Delicious or Royal Gala are best)
½ peeled **lime** (leave as much pith on as possible)
½ ripe **avocado** (organic if possible)
4 **ice cubes** or a small handful **crushed ice**

Juice the apples and lime. Add the flesh of the avocado to the blender along with the juice and ice. Blend – pour – enjoy!

Smoothie benefits Savoury Sweet contains vitamins A, B, B1, B2, B3, B6, C, E and K, folic acid, calcium, potassium, bioflavonoids, iron, magnesium, manganese, phosphorus, zinc, essential fats, pectin, malic acid, natural sugars and anti-oxidants. This smoothie will help alkaline the system, clean the colon and regulate the heart.

mangolicious

Mouth-watering **mango** and succulent **pineapple**, combined with **creamy** live **yogurt**

This recipe is smooth, succulent and scrummy!

½ juicy **mango**
⅓ medium **pineapple**
2 tablespoons low-fat live **yogurt**
1 small handful **ice**

Peel the mango and carefully cut the flesh away from the stone. Wash the pineapple and cut into chunks for juicing. Simply juice the pineapple (with the skin on) and pour into the blender with the mango, yogurt and ice. Blend – pour – enjoy!

Smoothie benefits By combining the flesh of the mango with the yogurt this creates a gorgeous, thick, creamy and filling smoothie. The live yogurt is bursting with friendly bacteria that furnish the intestine and fight bacterial infections as well as aid digestion. The delicious and aromatic mango is a terrific source of potassium and vitamins A and C.

turbo-charge smoothie

A truly amazing meal in a glass

Not only is this smoothie rich and incredibly creamy but it's also loaded with all six essential dietary needs. The blended avocado provides fibre and plenty of satisfying 'good' fat and protein. Packed with vitamins, minerals and antioxidants, this smoothie has been designed to nourish every cell in your body.

¼ **cucumber**
1 stick **celery**
½ small **pineapple**, peeled and chopped
1 handful **spinach** leaves
¼ **lime**, peeled
4 Golden Delicious **apples**, chopped
flesh of ½ ripe **avocado**
1 small handful crushed **ice**

Juice the cucumber, celery, pineapple, spinach, lime and 3½ apples. Place the avocado and the remaining ½ apple in a blender, together with the juice mixture and ice. Give a good whiz for 45 seconds. Pour into a glass and enjoy!

green power smoothie

Although similar to the Turbo-charge Smoothie, the addition of ginger, lemon, different apples and more celery makes a subtle change. Again, this is a meal in a glass, so take your time with it and drink only enough to make you full – don't think the more you drink the better because that's not how the body works.

2 sticks **celery**
½ small **cucumber**
3 Royal Gala **apples**
1 inch fresh **ginger**
2 cups **spinach**
½ small **pineapple**, peeled
½ **lemon**, peeled
1 ripe **avocado**
1 small handful crushed **ice**

Juice everything apart from the avocado and ice. Pour the juice into a blender along with the ice and avocado and give a good whiz. Pour into a glass and enjoy!

sunrise

Whether the morning sky is a lovely pink hue or whether clouds are blocking all hope of sunlight, this juice will emanate not only the colour but also the sunny feeling that is so often needed first thing. This juice is brimming with vitamins C and E, beta-carotene, calcium, potassium, folic acid and anti-oxidants. It's a great liver and kidney cleanser and a good energy enhancer. The sprinkle of wheat germ adds a boost of vitamins B and E and fibre.

1 **orange**, peeled
1 handful **strawberries**
3 **carrots**, topped and tailed
1 **lemon**, peeled
1 sprinkle **wheat germ**
1 handful crushed **ice**

Juice together the orange, strawberries, carrots and lemon. Once juiced, stir in the wheat germ and pour into a glass over ice. A beautiful array of sunshine colours to tantalize your taste buds!

turbo-charge weekend breakfast smoothie

This smoothie is packed with age-defying and disease-preventing anti-oxidants. It's a great breakfast smoothie, giving a good shot of vitamin C, and has a lovely crunchy consistency – good to get your teeth into!

1 small **pineapple**, peeled
2 handfuls **blueberries**
(or any berries you can get, fresh or frozen)

4 tablespoons live **yogurt**
1 handful soaked **almonds**
(best to soak overnight but not essential)

1 tablespoon organic **Manuka honey**

Juice the pineapple and 1 handful of the blueberries. Pour into a blender and whiz with the yogurt, remaining blueberries, nuts and honey until smooth. Pour into a glass and enjoy this beautiful and filling smoothie for breakfast.

energy boost

For best results, drink half an hour after your workout

For that simple injection of energy that is so often needed mid-afternoon, try reaching for this natural smoothie rather than for a chocolate bar. This smoothie will boost your energy naturally and satisfy any hunger pangs that may be starting to surface. It is also excellent if you are working out and looking to gain some muscle mass.

1 **mango**
½ medium **pineapple**
2 **dates**
1 **banana**
3 tablespoons live plain **yogurt**
1 teaspoon desiccated **coconut**
½ teaspoon organic **Manuka honey**
1 handful crushed **ice**

Peel the mango and cut the flesh around the stone. Peel
the pineapple and juice. Remove the stones from the dates.
Pour the pineapple juice into a blender along with all the
remaining ingredients. Give a good whiz, pour into a glass
and enjoy.

ultimate smoothie

Although **very filling**, this is **incredibly easy** for your **body** to **digest**

This really is the ultimate. Rich in beta-carotene, potassium, calcium, iron, zinc, chlorophyll, essential fats, good proteins and excellent carbohydrates, it's also brimming with anti-oxidants.

2 Golden Delicious **apples**
1 stick **celery**
2 **carrots**
½ cup **spinach**
½ cup **broccoli**
¼ **yellow pepper**
¼ **orange pepper**
⅛ **lime**, peeled
½ ripe **avocado**
½ handful crushed **ice**

Juice the apples, the celery, carrots, spinach, broccoli, peppers and lime. Place the avocado in a blender together with the juice and add the ice. Whiz for 1 minute, pour into a glass and enjoy!

Juicy Fruit Facts

Apple

Vitamins: A, B1, B2, B6, C

Minerals: calcium, chlorine, magnesium, phosphorus, potassium, sulphur, iron

Juicy extras: malic acid, pectin, ellagic acid

Juice or smoothie? juice — but can be used for fruit or vegetable smoothies;
can also be blended to thicken and add fibre to a smoothie

Good for ... anti-cancer health promoter; pectin forms a gel in the intestine that eliminates toxins

Apricot

Vitamins: B, C, beta-carotene

Minerals: sodium, potassium, magnesium, iron, calcium, silicon, boron

Juice or smoothie? smoothie

Good for ... energy, stamina, endurance; excellent blood builder; helping with heart disease; promoting shiny hair, glowing skin

Banana

Vitamins: B, C, beta-carotene, folic acid

Minerals: potassium, magnesium, calcium, sodium

Juice or smoothie: smoothie   !! **Warning — bananas do not juice !!**

Good for ... slow release energy; immune booster; staving off symptoms of PMS; helping lower cholestrol

Blueberry

Vitamins: B1, B2, B6, C, beta-carotene, folic acid

Minerals: calcium, iron, magnesium, manganese, phosphorus, potassium, sodium, zinc

Juicy extras: ellagic acid

Juice or smoothie? smoothie

Good for ... slowing down the signs of ageing; destroying free radicals

Blackcurrant

Vitamins: C, beta-carotene

Minerals: potassium, calcium, magnesium, phosphorus,

Juice or smoothie? smoothie – makes a wonderful, but expensive juice

Good for ... anti-cancer heath promoter; anti-bacterial; immune enhancer

Cherry

Vitamins: B, C, beta-carotene

Minerals: calcium, magnesium, zinc, iron, phosphorus, potassium, sulphur, copper, silicon

Juicy extras: pectin, ellagic acid

Juice or smoothie? smoothie – but makes a wonderful, but expensive juice

Good for ... anti-cancer health promoter; controlling blood cholesterol levels and pectin also forms a gel in the intestine that eliminates toxins

Cranberry

Vitamins: B, C, beta-carotene, folic acid

Minerals: iodine, calcium, chlorine, magnesium, phosphorus, potassium

Juicy extras: quinine

Juice or smoothie? juice or smoothie

Good for ... helping with liver, kidney, prostate or bladder problems

Grapefruit

Vitamins: C, beta-carotene

Minerals: calcium, potassium

Juicy extras: salicylic acid, pectin

Juice or smoothie? juice

Good for ... breaking down and shifting inorganic calcium from the joints; great at stimulating digestion

Grape

Vitamins: B, C, E, beta-carotene

Minerals: iron, calcium, phosphorus, potassium

Juicy extras: pectin

Juice or smoothie? juice

Good for ... helping to calm the nervous system; promoting good bowel movement; cleansing the system; restoring alkaline balance

Kiwi

Vitamins: C, E, beta-carotene

Minerals: calcium, magnesium, phosphorus, potassium, sodium

Juice or smoothie? juice or smoothie

Good for ... cleansing and energizing

Lemon/Lime

Vitamins: C, beta-carotene

Minerals: calcium, magnesium, phosphorus, potassium

Juicy extras: bioflavonoids, citric acid

Juice or smoothie? juice (add a small amount to other juices)

Good for ... cleansing the system – the acid scours the intestinal tract; eliminating toxins; neutralizing harmful bacteria

Mango

Vitamins: B, C, beta-carotene

Minerals: calcium, copper, magnesium, phosphorus, iron

Juice or smoothie? smoothie

Good for ... mopping up free radicals; internal body cleanser; stimulating the immune system; disinfecting the body and reducing body odour

Melon

Vitamins: A, C, folic acid

Minerals: calcium, zinc, potassium, magnesium, phosphorus

Juice or smoothie? juice (using the entire fruit)

Good for ... cooling the body; cleansing the kidneys; purifying the skin; promoting shiny hair, strong nails

Nectarine

Vitamins: B1, B2, B3, B5, B6, C, beta-carotene, folic acid

Minerals: calcium, magnesium, zinc, iron, phosphorus, potassium, copper

Juice or smoothie? smoothie – but makes a wonderful, if expensive juice

Good for ... anti-cancer health promoter and natural energizer

Orange

Vitamins: A, B6, C, beta-carotene, folic acid

Minerals: calcium, iron, potassium, phosphorus, zinc

Juicy extras: citric acid

Juice or smoothie? juice (leaving pith on)

Good for ... destroying free radicals that cause signs of skin ageing; scouring the intestine and flushing toxins from the body

Papaya

Vitamins: C, beta-carotene

Minerals: calcium, magnesium

Juicy extras: proteolytic enzymes

Juice or smoothie? smoothie

Good for ... enabling easy digestion of complex proteins; promotes male fertility

Peach

Vitamins: B3, C, beta-carotene, folic acid

Minerals: calcium, magnesium, zinc, iron, phosphorus, potassium, sulphur, copper, silicon

Juice or smoothie? smoothie – but makes a wonderful, if expensive juice

Good for ... fighting disease; anti-cancer health promoter; cleansing the intestine, bladder and kidneys

Pear

Vitamins: B6, C

Minerals: copper, potassium

Juice or smoothie? juice

Good for ... controlling diabetes: contains levulose – a fruit sugar more easily tolerated by people with diabetes

Pineapple

Vitamins: B, C, E, folic acid

Minerals: potassium, iron, calcium, sodium, phosphorus

Juicy extras: bromeline

Juice or smoothie? juice – but can be used for fruit or vegetable smoothies; can also be blended to add thickness and fibre to a smoothie

Good for ... bromeline is an enzyme that aids digestion and helps dissolve excess mucus so is useful for hay fever and asthma

Raspberry

Vitamins: B, C, E, beta-carotene, niacin

Minerals: calcium, iron, potassium, magnesium, phosphorus, sodium, zinc

Juicy extras: ellagic acid

Juice or smoothie? smoothie

Good for ... maintaining healthy male reproductive function; promoting healthy skin; slowing down the signs of ageing

Strawberry

Vitamins: B, C, E, beta-carotene, folic acid, niacin

Minerals: calcium, potassium, iron, sodium, magnesium, phosphorus, sulphur, zinc

Juicy extras: ellagic acid

Juice or smoothie? smoothie – but makes a wonderful, if expensive juice

Good for ... building blood; boosting the immune system; slowing down the signs of ageing

Juicy Vegetable Facts

Avocado

Vitamins: B, C, beta-carotene

Minerals: potassium, calcium, iron, phosphorus

Juicy extras: essential natural fats

Juice or smoothie? smoothie !! **Warning – avocados do not juice !!**

Good for ... a balanced diet: contains all 6 human nutritional needs in abundance – water, fat, protein, natural sugar, vitamins and minerals

Beetroot

Vitamins: B, C, beta-carotene, folic acid

Minerals: chlorine, manganese, calcium, iron, sodium, phosphorus, potassium, chromium, magnesium

Juicy extras: although a veg, it tastes sweet

Juice or smoothie? juice

Good for ... cleansing the liver; iron deficiency anaemia; helping reduce hardening and blockage of the arteries

Broccoli

Vitamins: B, C, beta-carotene, folic acid

Minerals: calcium, iron, phosphorus, potassium, sulphur

Juice or smoothie? juice

Good for ... high blood pressure; liver problems; constipation

Carrot

Vitamins: B, C, E, K, beta-carotene

Minerals: calcium, iron, phosphorus, potassium, sulphur, chromium, magnesium, sodium, iodine, silica

Juicy extras: although a veg, it tastes sweet

Juice or smoothie? juice

Good for ... promoting healthy eyes; skin problems; cleansing the liver

Celery

Vitamins: B, C

Minerals: calcium, iron, phosphorus, potassium, sulphur, sodium

Juice or smoothie? juice

Good for ... reducing acidity, so useful for arthritis and gout; natural diuretic; reducing fluid retention; calming the nervous system

Cucumber

Vitamins: B, C, beta-carotene

Minerals: sodium, silica, manganese, sulphur, potassium, calcium, phosphorus, chlorine, magnesium

Juice or smoothie? juice

Good for ... excellent diuretic; reducing fluid retention; superb for the hair, nails and skin; helping reduce blood pressure

Fennel

Vitamins: B, C, beta-carotene

Minerals: calcium, chromium, cobalt, iron, magnesium, manganese, phosphorus, potassium, selenium, silicon, sodium, zinc

Juice or smoothie? juice

Good for ... reducing intestinal gas, flatulence and bloating; calming effect on digestion

Ginger

Vitamins: C

Minerals: copper, potassium, sodium, iron, calcium, zinc, phosphorus, magnesium

Juice or smoothie? juice

Good for ... natural antibiotic and decongestant

Parsnip

Vitamins: C, K, folic acid

Minerals: potassium, iron, calcium, manganese

Juice or smoothie? juice

Good for ... helping to reduce blood pressure

Peppers

Vitamins: B, C, beta-carotene, folic acid

Minerals: potassium, silica, iron, calcium, phosphorus, magnesium

Juice or smoothie? juice

Good for ... cleansing liver and intestine

Spinach

Vitamins: B, C, K, beta-carotene, folic acid

Minerals: iron, iodine, calcium, phosphorus, potassium, sulphur

Juice or smoothie? juice

Good for ... anaemia – supporting effective liver and kidney function

Tomato

Vitamins: B, C, K

Minerals: potassium, calcium, iron, phosphorus, iodine

Juicy extras: lycopene

Juice or smoothie? juice or smoothie

Good for ... helpful for high blood pressure; cleansing the liver; lycopene has renowned anti-cancer properties

Watercress

Vitamins: B, C, E, beta-carotene, folic acid

Minerals: sulphur, calcium, iron, sodium, magnesium, phosphorus, chlorine, potassium, iodine

Juice or smoothie? juice

Good for ... cleansing the liver; reducing fluid retention; healthy kidney function

juicy info

For more information on the Juice Booster range, Juice Master books, CDs, DVDs, forthcoming seminars, juice-bar opportunities, plus anything else you need to know about our juicy world, please contact us at:

Juice Master Hotline: **08451 30 28 29**
(this is a local call charge from anywhere in the UK)

Website: **www.juicemaster.com**

E-mail: **info@juicemaster.com**

The Juice Master's Mind and Body Detox Retreats

Fancy an amazing experience? Why not spend a week in a beautiful European coastal destination, drinking only the finest-quality freshly extracted juices, doing yoga, meditation, meeting new people and attending seminars designed to change the way you think about what you feed yourself? These are only held a few times a year, so places go fast. For more info, see the website or speak to one of the juicy team. Use the juicy vouchers to get you started!

Happy juicing!

£75 OFF	**£75 OFF**
1-Week Detox Retreat	3-Day Juice/Spa Detox

Note: The money off vouchers are not in conjunction with any other offer.